CHRISTMAS

HISTORY
PROPHECY
THE NATIVITY

Amanda Bennett

This book belongs to

_____

All Scripture quotations, unless otherwise noted, are taken from the Holy Bible, King James Version.

Christmas:
History, Prophecy, The Nativity

ISBN 1-888306-13-0

Copyright © 1996 by Amanda Bennett

Published by:
Homeschool Press
255 S. Bridge St.
P.O. Box 254
Elkton, MD 21922-0254

Send requests for information to the above address.

Homeschool Press is an imprint of Holly Hall Publications.

Cover design by Mark Dinsmore.

Printed in the United States of America.

This book is dedicated to my children,
who have helped me focus on the true meaning
of Christmas—the fulfillment of God's promise
through the Birth of the Saviour!

How To Use This Guide

Welcome to the world of unit studies! They present a wonderful method of learning for all ages and it is a great pleasure to share this unit study with you. This guide has been developed and written to provide a basic framework for the study, along with plenty of ideas and resources to help round out the learning adventure.

TO BEGIN: The **Outline** is the study "skeleton", providing an overall view of the subject and important subtopics. It can be your starting point—read through it and familiarize yourself with the content. It is great for charting your course over the next few weeks (or developing lesson plans). Please understand that you do not necessarily have to proceed through the outline in order. I personally focus on the areas that our children are interested in first—giving them "ownership" of the study. By beginning with their interest areas, it gives us the opportunity to further develop these interests while stretching into other areas of the outline as they increase their topic knowledge.

By working on a unit study for five or six weeks at a time, you can catch the children's attention and hold it for valuable learning. I try to wrap up each unit study in five or six weeks, whether or not we have "completed" the unit outline. The areas of the outline that we did not yet cover may be covered the next time we delve into the unit study topic (in a few months or perhaps next year). These guides are **non-consumable**—you can use them over and over again, covering new areas of interest as you review the previous things learned in the process.

The **Reading** and **Reference Lists** are lists of resources that feed right into various areas of the **Outline**. The books are listed with grade level recommendations and all the information that you need to locate them in the library or from your favorite book retailer. You can also order them through the national Inter-Library Loan System (I.L.L.)—check with the reference librarian at your local library.

There are several other components that also support the unit study. They include:

The **Spelling and Vocabulary Lists** identify words that apply directly to the unit study, and are broken down into both Upper and Lower Levels for use with several ages.

The **Suggested Software, Games and Videos List** includes games, software and videos that make the learning fun, while reinforcing some of the basic concepts studied.

The **Activities and Field Trip List** include specific activity materials and field trip ideas that can be used with this unit to give some hands-on learning experience.

The **Internet Resources List** identifies stops on the information super-highway that will open up brand new learning opportunities.

The author and the publisher care about you and your family. While not all of the materials recommended in this guide are written from a Christian perspective, they all have great educational value. Please use caution when using any materials. It's important to take the time to review books, games, and internet sites before your children use them to make sure they meet your family's expectations.

As you can see, all of these sections have been included to help you build your unit study into a fun and fruitful learning adventure. Unit studies provide an excellent learning tool and give the students lifelong memories about the topic and the study.

The left-hand pages of this book have been filled with new and exciting things which will help bring this study to life for your family.

"Have fun & Enjoy the Adventure!"

Table of Contents

Introduction

Christmas, a time of praise and rejoicing, is quickly approaching. It is time to ready our hearts and homes as well as our minds for this special Christian holiday! It is a time of beautiful sights and sounds, family worship and traditions. From the smells of cinnamon and cloves, the sight of twinkling lights and beautiful nativity scenes to the radiant faces of the children, Christmas opens the door to our faith as well as our hearts. As we celebrate His birth, let us take time to learn and share this love that God packaged so carefully and sent to us on that night so long ago in a small town called Bethlehem. Like the shepherds and the wise men, we, too, still seek Him!

Just as the stars lit the sky on that night so long ago, we can use this study to light our way back to that time, to walk the streets of Bethlehem and stand in its olive groves. Using this unit study and some good books and videos, we can visit the places and see the sights. We can study the history of the Roman government as well as the tyranny of Herod, who was put in his position with the help of none other than Cleopatra and Mark Antony!

In this study, you will learn what the world was like when Christ was born, what the Romans and Jews were facing, as well as learning more about His birth. It was the fulfillment of hundreds of years of anticipation from prophecies of old. This will give you and your children a more complete picture of the event as well as its significance, the coming of the King. There are many earthly and material things that keep obscuring the true meaning of Christmas, but this study will help bring the focus back to the reason for the season, which is the birth of Jesus.

It is my prayer that you learn from this as we are learning. Close your eyes and envision the brightness of that star in the heavens almost 2,000 years ago—can't you see the anticipation and eagerness on the faces of the Wise Men? Like those weary travelers, we, too, seek the King as we approach the celebration of His birth. Each year, when we work on this study, we understand more and are blessed in many ways. We tend to share our new knowledge with those around us, who tend to share and on and on, like a pebble dropped in the ocean, or the birth of a tiny baby so long ago in Bethlehem, who knows how far the ripples will travel? No one birth or event in the history of mankind has even come close to making such an impact on all people of all countries! Use this study of Christmas as a wonderful opportunity to learn more about Jesus, as well as a time to reach out and share with others.

Hallelujah, Christ is born!

*"And, lo, the angel of the Lord came upon them,
and the glory of the Lord shone round about them:
and they were sore afraid. And the angel said unto them,
Fear not: for, behold, I bring you good tidings of great joy,
which shall be to all people. For unto you is born this day
in the city of David a Saviour, which is Christ the Lord.*

*And this shall be a sign unto you; Ye shall find the babe
wrapped in swaddling clothes, lying in a manger. And suddenly
there was with the angel a multitude of the heavenly host
praising God, and saying,*

Glory to God in the highest, and on earth peace, good will toward men."

Luke 2:9-14 (KJV)

Sign of the TIMES

2166-2000 B.C.

NOTE FROM AUTHOR AND PUBLISHER: An asterisk (*) denotes an approximate date for use in your timeline. There are many schools of thought regarding the exact date of many Biblical events. The items listed are done so to give you and your students a picture of the sheer expanse of time that passed while the Israelites awaited their Messiah. Sometimes centuries passed between prophecies! Each of the first three pages of the timeline cover a millennium of time, while the next six cover twenty-five years per page. **Enjoy the Adventure!**

2166* —Abram born
2091* —Abram (Abraham) moves to Canaan
2066* —Isaac born
2006* —Jacob and Esau born

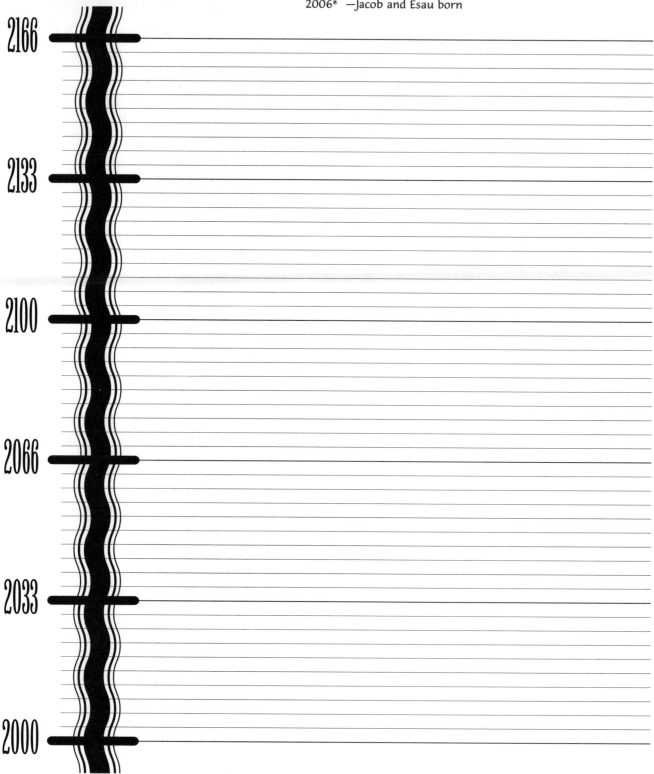

2166

2133

2100

2066

2033

2000

Unit Study Outline

I. Introduction

A. Reason for the holiday, the birth of our Lord!
   1. With His birth came the light of the world, the promise of our future
   2. God became man on that night so long ago, in the form of a helpless tiny infant
B. Impact of the holiday on times of yesterday and today
   1. Christians celebrate His birth with worship and praise
   2. Much of the world stops and rests, taking notice of Christians and their faith
   3. Even our days are measured by His birth, as our calendar (Gregorian) is based on time *"anno Domini"* (A.D.) since His coming
C. Many lessons to be learned through the study of this holiday and Christ's birth
   1. Strengthens our faith by making us aware of God's power and plan, seeing His timing and love throughout history
   2. Introduces us to history at that special time in civilization, the spread of power, the development of kingdoms, and particularly the eventual spread of Christianity
   3. Provides a wonderful opportunity to learn more about the Jews, the earthly race that God chose for His Son—their faith and their lives at the time of His birth

II. Life in the time of Jesus' birth

A. Government of Judea, a Roman province
   1. Herod, King of Judea at Christ's birth, was put into power by the Roman government
      a. In the year 40 B.C., Herod was driven from Palestine by Parthians seeking to control Judea
      b. Fleeing, he journeyed to Egypt, seeking help to get to Rome for assistance
         (1) Cleopatra, seeing his military abilities, offered Herod a command in her army
         (2) Refusing her offer, Herod continued on to Rome with Cleopatra's assistance and a personal referral to Mark Antony

SIGN OF THE TIMES

1999-1000 B.C.

Here are some interesting events to include on YOUR timeline! Then, add on the important dates and events that you learn from your study of Christmas from this era . . .

1915*	—Joseph born
1898*	—Joseph sold into slavery
1526*	—Moses born
1445*	—The exodus of Israelites from Egypt
1105*	—Samuel born
1050-1010*	—Rule of Saul of a united kingdom
1010-970*	—Rule of David of a united kingdom

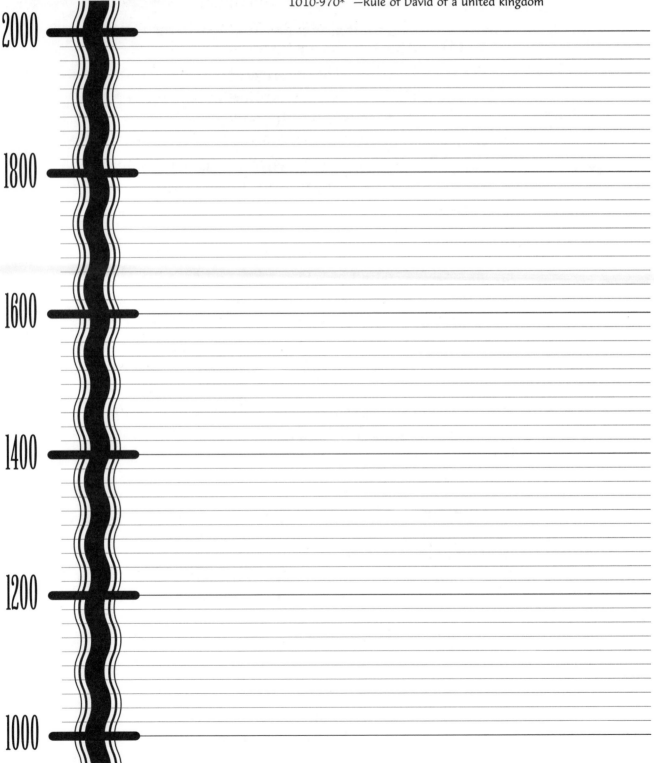

2000

1800

1600

1400

1200

1000

c.　Arriving in Rome, Herod sought help from Mark Antony, an old family friend
　　　　　(1)　Antony, seeing the value of Herod in Palestine, appeared before the Senate to recommend that Herod be made King
　　　　　(2)　The Senate agreed with Antony and passed a decree that made Herod the King of Judea
　　　　　(3)　Accompanied by both Antony and Octavian (soon to be Caesar Augustus), Herod was given his new title. He was also given troops to go back and claim Jerusalem for Rome
　　　　　(4)　In the 37 B.C., Herod and his Roman soldiers successfully attacked Jerusalem and took over control of Palestine for Rome
　　2.　Herod, a tyrant ruler
　　　a.　Herod was half Jew (not by ancestry, but by conversion) and half Arab, and was very much hated by the Jews of Judea
　　　b.　It is said that Herod was often controlled by demons, tortured and paranoid for most of his time as a ruler
　　　c.　Herod was known to be merciless, killing his own wife, children, family members and many others
　　　d.　Herod ruled Palestine for approximately 33 years (37 BC to 4 BC)
B.　Daily life of the Israelites
　　1.　Family life
　　　a.　Life revolved around the family
　　　b.　The husband was the family leader, both spiritually and legally
　　　c.　The husband was also the provider for his wife and children, and early religious educator, as well
　　　d.　The wife was responsible for the home, cleaning the home, watching the children, making clothing, bringing water from the well and preparing food
　　　e.　The families observed the Sabbath as a day of rest and worship, as well as keeping other holy days

Sign of the TIMES

999-0 B.C.

Here are some interesting events to include on YOUR timeline! Then, add on the important dates and events that you learn from your study of Christmas from this era . . .

970-930* —Rule of Solomon of a united kingdom
750-686* —Ministry of Micah
740-681* —Ministry of Isaiah, etc.
520-480* —Ministry of Zechariah
440-430* —Ministry of Malachi
432-5* —Time between Old and New Testaments

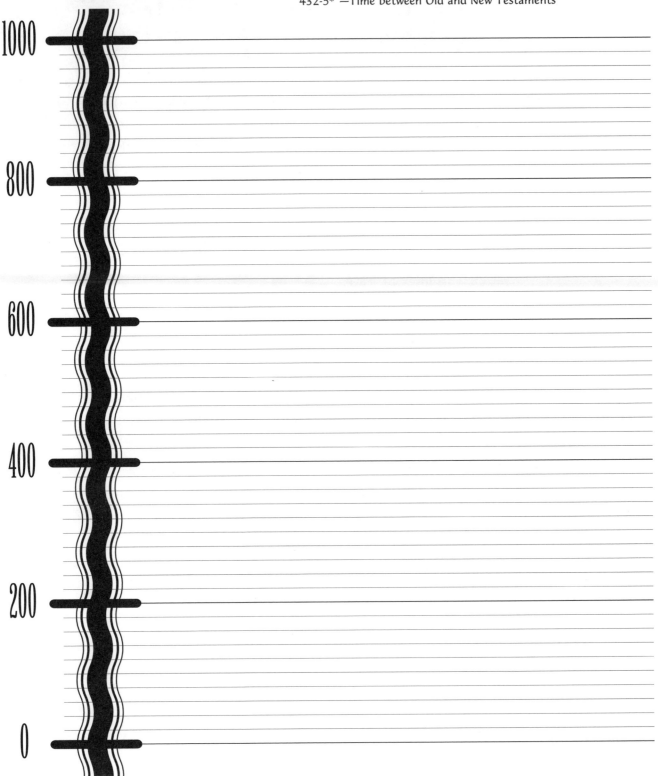

2. Education and religion
   a. To Jews, education and religion went hand in hand, and were woven throughout their daily lives
   b. Children were taught at an early age about their religion, through observation on the Sabbath, as well as instruction at home
   c. Boys, at the age of five, began school, attending six days a week, usually at the synagogue
3. Economic life
   a. Villages had farmers as well as tradesmen among their residents
   b. The tradesmen included carpenters, weavers, leather crafters and blacksmiths
   c. Trade in the village usually involved bartering services for food and other items

C. Religion
   1. The Jewish faith was a focal point in their lives; everything revolved around their faith and its applications to daily life
   2. The Jews were the chosen people of God
   3. Persecuted, overthrown and ruled over, they awaited the arrival of a King who had been promised for hundreds and hundreds of years
   4. The Torah was the record of their faith and its meaning, while the synagogue was their central place of worship

D. The Roman Empire
   1. At the time of Jesus' birth, Caesar Augustus was the first emperor of Rome
   2. The Empire consisted of the countries around the Mediterranean Sea, including Egypt, Judea, Greece, Macedonia, Italy, France (Gaul) and Spain
   3. The most powerful empire on earth at that time, Rome controlled vast territories and many people of numerous nationalities
   4. The Romans built roads, improved trade routes and developed many other technological advances in their time
   5. Trade included items such as cloth, spices, olive oil, precious metals, glass, lumber, wine and grain

Sign of the TIMES

50-25 B.C.

Here are some interesting events to include on YOUR timeline! Then, add on the important dates and events that you learn from your study of Christmas from this era . . .

46 —Africa is made a Roman province
46 —Leap year is introduced into the Julian Calendar
39 —Herod is named king of the Jews by Rome with the help of Mark Antony
31 —Egypt is made a Roman province
30 —Construction is begun on the Pantheon

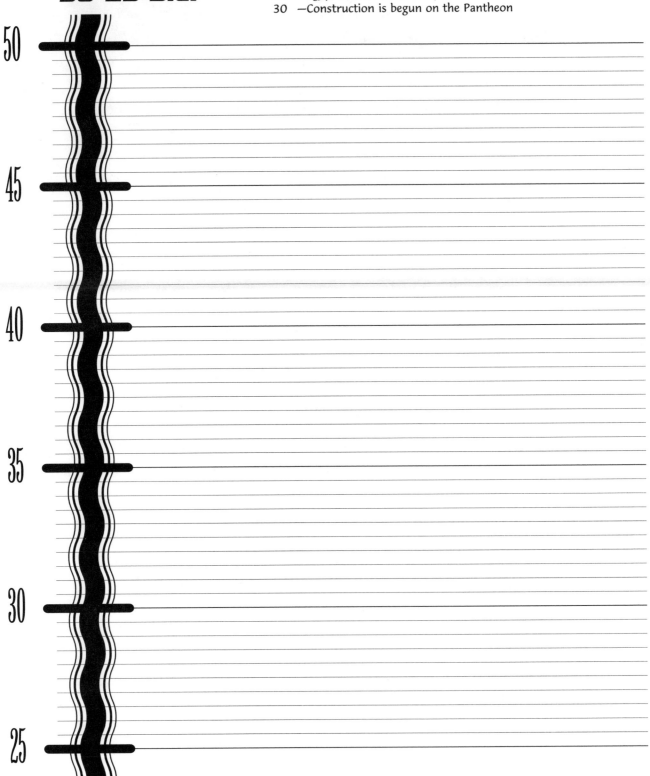

50

45

40

35

30

25

III. Preparing for the birth of Christ in Israel

A. The Israelites had been waiting for centuries for the promised Savior

B. They had studied and learned the prophecies of His birth (quoted here from the Old Testament of the King James Version (KJV) of the Bible)

   1. His birth is promised: "For unto us a child is born, unto us a son is given: and the government shall be upon his shoulder: and his name shall be called Wonderful, Counsellor, The mighty God, The everlasting Father, The Prince of Peace." Isaiah 9:6

   2. He would be born of a virgin: "Therefore the Lord himself shall give you a sign; Behold, a virgin shall conceive, and bear a son, and shall call his name Immanuel." Isaiah 7:14

   3. He would be from the tribe of Judah: "The sceptre shall not depart from Judah, nor a lawgiver from between his feet, until Shiloh come; and unto him shall the gathering of the people be." Genesis 49:10

   4. He would be born in Bethlehem: "But thou, Bethlehem Ephratah, though thou be little among the thousands of Judah, yet out of thee shall he come forth unto me that is to be ruler of Israel; whose goings forth have been from of old, from everlasting." Micah 5:2

   5. He would be worshipped by the Magi: "Thus saith the Lord, the Redeemer of Israel, and his Holy One, to him whom man despiseth, to him whom the nation abhorreth, to a servant of rulers, Kings shall see and arise, princes also shall worship…" Isaiah 49:7

   6. The Magi shall bring gifts: "The multitude of camels shall cover thee, the dromedaries of Midian and Ephah; all they from Sheba shall come: they shall bring gold and incense; and they shall shew forth the praises of the Lord." Isaiah 60:6

C. They probably expected a king; one that was physically powerful and could demolish the Romans and other tyrants and save them from their misery

D. They were not expecting a tiny helpless baby, born almost unnoticed, heralded only by angels and shepherds from the fields

Sign of the Times

25-0 B.C.

Here are some interesting events to include on YOUR timeline! Then, add on the important dates and events that you learn from your study of Christmas from this era . . .

18	—Herod begins rebuilding the temple
6	—Rome annexes Judaea
6/5*	—Jesus Christ is born
4	—Herod dies

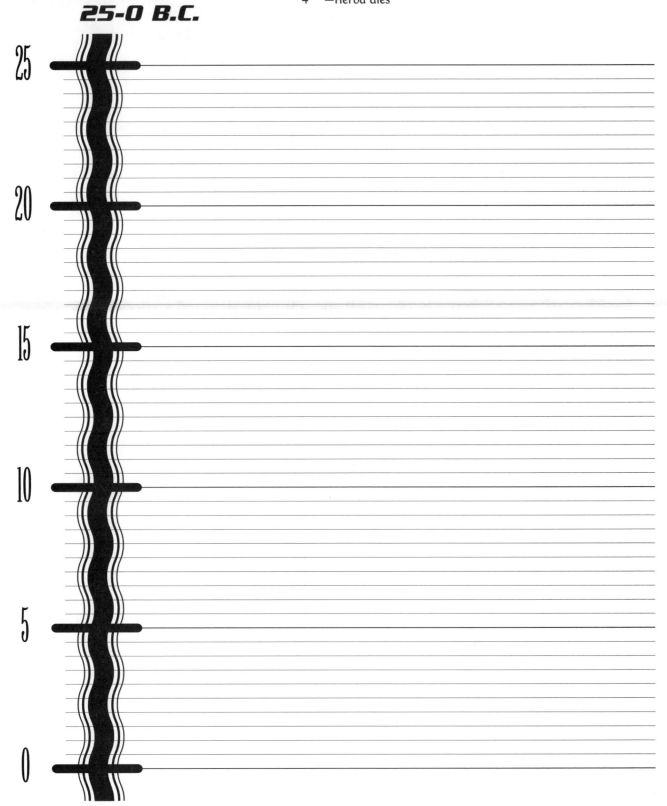

25

20

15

10

5

0

IV. The Birth of Jesus Christ, Son of God

A. The announcement of the upcoming birth of John the Baptist
   1. Zacharias is visited by the angel Gabriel, telling him of the son that he and Elisabeth would soon have
   2. Elisabeth, Mary's cousin, conceives, in her advanced years
   3. John the Baptist is born, a few months before Jesus, growing to serve God and prepare the way for Jesus' ministry

B. The announcement of the upcoming birth of Jesus to Mary
   1. The angel Gabriel also visited Mary, in the city of Nazareth, when Elisabeth was six months pregnant
      a. Gabriel told Mary that God had found favor with her, and that she would conceive the Son of God and that His name would be Jesus
      b. The angel also told Mary the news of Elisabeth's pregnancy
      c. Mary accepted the angel's news, saying "..be it unto me according to thy word." (Luke 1:38)
   2. Mary went to visit Elisabeth, sharing the news from the angel

C. The announcement of the birth to Joseph
   1. Joseph, learning of Mary's pregnancy, considered putting her away privately to avoid making her a public example
   2. In a dream, the angel of the Lord reassured Joseph about Mary and the baby
      a. The angel instructed Joseph to go ahead and take Mary as his wife
      b. The angel explained that Mary's baby was conceived of the Holy Spirit, and was to be called Jesus, and that He would save His people from their sins
   3. Arising from his dream, Joseph did as the angel instructed, taking Mary as his wife

D. Joseph and Mary travel from their home in Nazareth to Bethlehem
   1. A decree was sent out from Caesar Augustus, stating that all the world should be taxed, having everyone return to the town of their birth to enroll for the tax

SIGN OF THE TIMES

0-25 A.D.

Here are some interesting events to include on YOUR timeline! Then, add on the important dates and events that you learn from your study of Christmas from this era . . .

5/6* —Christ in the temple at age twelve
14 —Augustus Caesar dies

0

5

10

15

20

25

2. Born in Bethlehem, Joseph took Mary and travelled with her to the place of his birth
   a. The journey covered approximately 90 miles, which was a long trip in those days (about a five-day walk), especially with a woman in such a late stage of pregnancy
   b. One of the prophecies that they had learned as children stated that the King would be from Bethlehem; this thought must have both excited them as well as scared them a bit as they made their way back to Bethlehem
   c. Bethlehem was located on a low rocky ridge just south of Jerusalem, surrounded by olive groves and fertile fields

E. After arriving in Bethlehem, they found that there was no room for them in the inn (also known as a caravansary—a resting place for caravans of travelers)
   1. In the time of enrollment, there were probably crowds of people in the town, making it difficult to find a room for them to stay in during their visit
   2. They probably stayed in a stable or a cave on the outskirts of town, where animals were oftentimes kept in the evening

F. While in Bethlehem, the days were accomplished that Mary should deliver her firstborn Son!
   1. Jesus was born there in Bethlehem, wrapped in swaddling clothes and laid in a manger
      a. Swaddling clothes were usually made by the mother-to-be for her new baby, and were used to bind the newborn baby's limbs
      b. A manger was the word used to refer to an animal feed trough, usually made of wood or carved into the wall of a cave
   2. With His birth, Jesus fulfilled the prophecies of old, being born of a virgin in Bethlehem, from the line of David.

G. Meanwhile, out in the fields surrounding Bethlehem, an angel of the Lord appeared to shepherds that were guarding their flocks through the night
   1. The angel explained to them that the Savior had been born that day, in the city of David (Bethlehem)

SIGN OF THE TIMES

25-50 A.D..

Here are some interesting events to include on YOUR timeline! Then, add on the important dates and events that you learn from your study of Christmas from this era . . .

27* —Jesus is baptized
30* —Jesus is crucified
35* —Paul (Saul) converted to Christianity
40* —Christian Church is built in Corinth
43 —City of London is founded
45 —Paul begins his missionary travels
47 —The Greek historian Plutarch is born

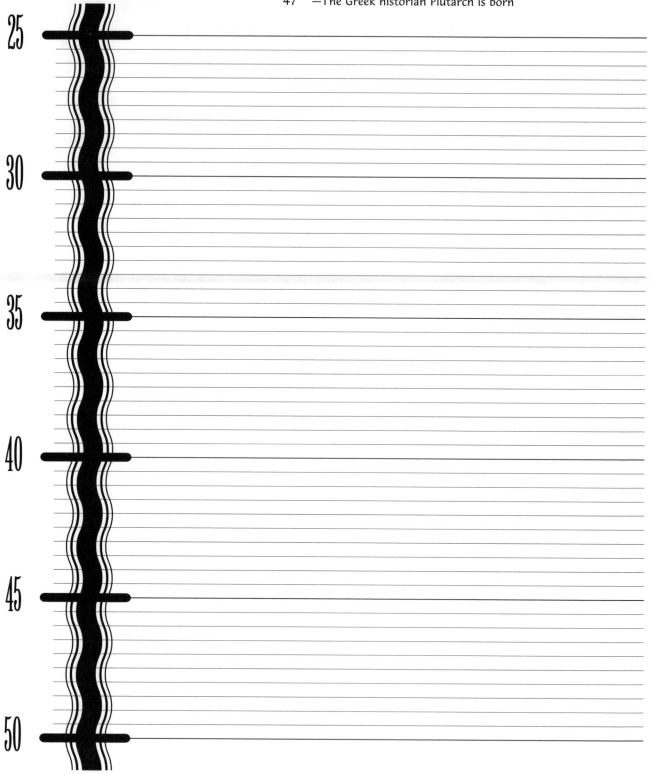

25

30

35

40

45

50

2. The angel also told them that they would find the baby wrapped in swaddling clothes, lying in a manger

3. Afraid of the angel at first, the shepherds heard the words in awe

4. After telling the shepherds of the news of Jesus' birth, the angel was joined by a multitude of angels that were praising God, saying "Glory to God in the highest, and on earth peace, good will toward men." (Luke 2:14)

5. After the angels were gone, the shepherds decided to go into Bethlehem to find this baby

6. Hastening to Bethlehem, the shepherds found the baby lying in a manger

7. After finding the babe, they departed, glorifying and praising God for all that they had seen

V. Jesus is presented to the world

A. Mary and Joseph travelled with baby Jesus to the temple of Jerusalem, when He was approximately 40 days old, in accordance with Jewish laws

1. Mary's period of separation after the birth of the baby was over and they travelled to Jerusalem for the rites of purification

2. Baby Jesus was presented for redemption before God, remembering His protection of Israel's firstborn sons as they fled Egypt

B. While at the temple, they were met by a man named Simeon

1. Simeon had been assured by the Holy Ghost that he would not die until he had seen Jesus, and he recognized the Savior, as Joseph and Mary entered the temple

2. Taking Jesus in his arms and blessing God, Simeon said of Jesus, "A light to lighten the Gentiles, and the glory of thy people Israel." (Luke 2:32)

C. Also at the temple was Anna, a prophetess of great age

1. She had prayed and fasted for years at the temple

2. She, too, recognized the Savior as they were in the temple, and thanked God for Him

3. Anna then shared the news of the Savior with others who visited the temple for redemption

SIGN OF THE TIMES

50-75 A.D.

Here are some interesting events to include on YOUR timeline! Then, add on the important dates and events that you learn from your study of Christmas from this era . . .

50-52	—Paul's second missionary journey
51/52*	—1, 2 Thessalonians written to the church at Thessalonica
53-57	—Paul's third missionary journey
57	—Romans written to the church at Rome
59-61/62*	—Paul imprisoned in Rome
66/67*	—2 Timothy written

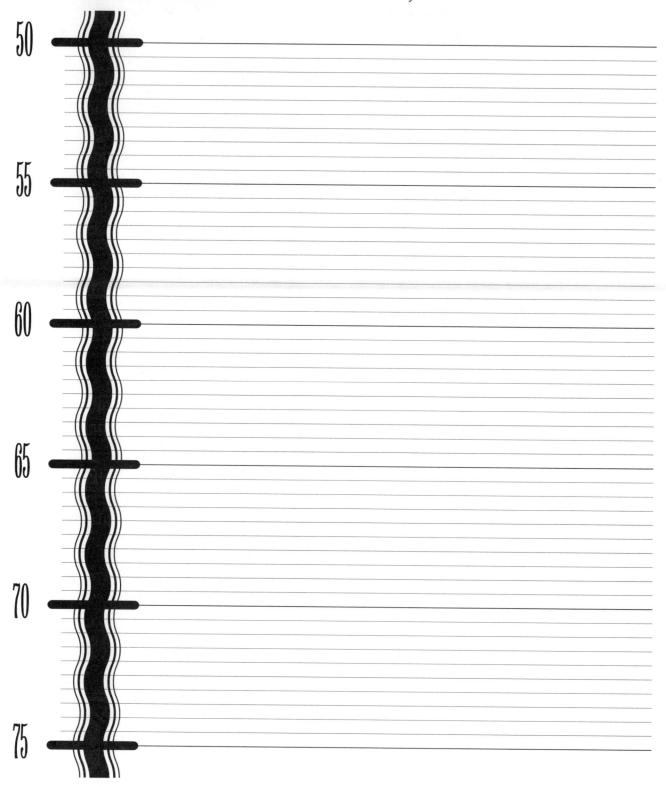

50

55

60

65

70

75

D. Some time in the first two years of His life, Jesus was visited by wise men from the East
    1. They had followed a bright star to Jerusalem, and were asking the whereabouts of the King of the Jews
    2. Their questions got the attention of Herod, who considered himself to be King of the Jews
        a. Herod brought the wise men to meet with him privately, and asked questions about their knowledge of this King
        b. After inquiring of his scribes and priests as to the location of where the "Christ" would be born, Herod sent the wise men to Bethlehem, asking them to return and tell him where the baby was so that he, too, could go and worship the King
    3. The wise men journeyed on to Bethlehem, following the bright star as it went before them, and brought them to the young child, Jesus
        a. They fell down and worshipped Him
        b. They presented him with treasures fit for a king (gold, frankincense and myrrh)
        c. Being warned in a dream to not return to Herod, the wise men left for their country another way
    4. Herod, after determining that he had been tricked by the Wise Men, ordered that all children under two years old were to be killed
    5. Joseph took Mary and Jesus and fled to Egypt, after being warned in dream about Herod's plan to have the child destroyed

VI. History of the holiday

A. Early Christians
    1. Evidence of the earliest celebration of the Nativity was found in paintings on the walls of the catacombs, where early Christians worshiped in safety
    2. As Paul and others spread the Christian faith, the churches became established, and Romans were converted to Christianity
    3. By 135 A.D., Christians began to assemble to sing the angels' hymns on the Holy Night of the Nativity

SIGN OF THE TIMES

Here are some interesting events to include on YOUR timeline! Then, add on the important dates and events that you learn from your study of Christmas from this era . . .

79-81 —Titus emperor of Roman Empire
90-95* —John exiled on Patmos
95* —The book of Revelation written

75-100 A.D.

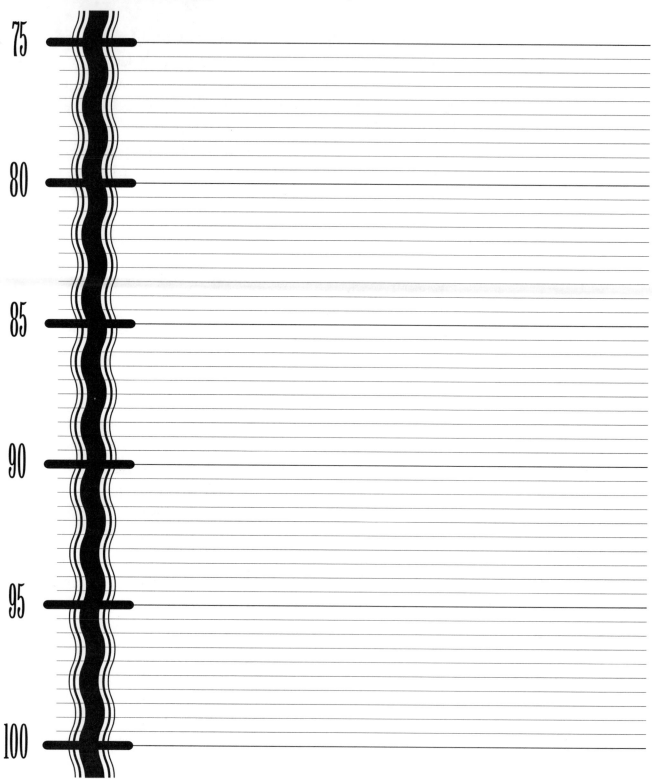

75

80

85

90

95

100

4.   In the year 312 A.D., Emperor Constantine made Christianity the religion of Rome

B.   The early Church
    1.   The Church, trying to draw in more people to Christianity and away from the worship of false gods, made an effort to identify various Christian holidays
    2.   The Church established the Feast of the Nativity, or celebration of Christ's birth, on December 25th
        a.   The church frequently timed Christian holidays to coincide with the pagan festivities, to help the people make an easier transition to Christianity
        b.   Pope Julius I (337 - 352 A.D.), in an effort to honor the birth of Jesus, had extensive research performed to try to establish the date of His birth
        c.   Prior to this time, Christmas had been celebrated with Epiphany on January 6
        d.   There are many different explanations of the choice of December 25th as the date of Christmas, varying from pagan roots to tax records of Rome, etc.
    3.   With his own conversion to Christianity, Emperor Theodosius I, in 374 A.D., outlawed all pagan festivities, including the Olympics as well as the celebration of Saturnalia and other pagan festivities that occurred at the end of the year

C.   The Middle Ages
    1.   With the spread of Christianity throughout Europe, so went the celebration of Christmas and other Christian observances
    2.   Depending on the government or ruler of the time, the celebration of Christmas waxed and waned from times of religious worship and praise to times of eating and wild festivities

D.   The Reformation
    1.   King Henry VIII formed a new church, the Church of England, breaking away from the Roman Catholic Church
    2.   With the Reformation came great changes in the church, helped along by famous figures such as Martin Luther, John Knox, etc., forming the foundation of the Protestant church
    3.   The Puritans and Separatists refused to worship according to the dictates of King Henry VIII and the leaders that followed him; they did not celebrate Christmas, as it was looked upon as having associations with the rituals and traditions of the King's Church as well as having its roots in pagan festivities

Favorite Christmas
Recipes

Does your mother or grandmother have a favorite Christmas dish or dessert that you enjoy each year? Ask them for the recipe—or better yet, ask them to show you how to make it! Enjoy shopping for the ingredients, and then enjoy eating the results. Here's an idea: make an extra batch or portion to share with a friend or neighbor!

My Favorite Christmas Recipe

E. Colonization of America
   1. This defiance towards celebrating Christmas was brought to America by the Puritans and Separatists
   2. In the early years of colonization, it was actually against the law to celebrate Christmas in some parts of this country
   3. As more and more people from other parts of Europe came to settle in the United States, they brought their own special Christian celebrations of Christmas with them
F. Christmas becomes a holiday in America
   1. In 1836, Alabama was the first state to declare Christmas a legal holiday, soon to be followed by all of the other states
   2. Celebrated in many ways throughout the country, Christmas has become a favorite holiday across the nation
   3. Like any other holiday or political idea or human effort, Christmas can be viewed from many perspectives
      a. Some choose to celebrate the holiday to observe the real reason for the season, the birth of our Lord
      b. Others choose to celebrate the season for both religious reasons, as well as observing other family traditions
      c. In this materialistic world that we live in, some choose to celebrate the holiday just for a day off from work, a time of gathering family together and a time of revelry

VII. The Christian celebration of Christmas includes many different traditions and events, with the central theme being the birth of Christ

A. Advent is a holy time of the seasons that some celebrate, a time of fasting and prayer, preparing hearts for the coming of the King
   1. Advent begins on the fourth Sunday before Christmas
   2. The days of Advent are marked with special daily devotions, weekly services and calendars
B. Some families celebrate the twelve days of Christmas, which begin on Christmas Eve and continue until January 6th, the celebration of Epiphany (the celebration of the Wise Men's visit)
C. Christmas is also the time that we hear and sing beautiful carols that praise God for sending His Son (look up some of the history of these carols—they have some fascinating stories!)
   1. *Silent Night*
   2. *Away in a Manger*

Write Your Own Christmas Song

Have you ever laughed at some silly song about Christmas that uses a familiar melody, but replaces the words? Try your hand at creating your own song about Christmas! Suggestion: use a secular tune for a "silly song" —or for a serious song, try borrowing the melody from a classic carol.

Write a Song About Christmas

Title: _____

Tune: _____

_____
_____
_____
_____
_____
_____
_____
_____
_____
_____
_____
_____
_____
_____
_____
_____
_____
_____

3. *O Little Town of Bethlehem*
4. *Joy to the World*
5. *O Come, All Ye Faithful*
6. *Good Christian Men Rejoice*
7. *The First Noël*
8. *Angels We Have Heard on High*
9. *Angels From the Realms of Glory*
10. *Hark! The Herald Angels Sing*
11. *It Came Upon a Midnight Clear*
12. *We Three Kings of Orient Are*
13. *What Child is This?*
14. *O Holy Night*

D. Many American families celebrate this beautiful day with the same types of activities
1. Time is spent attending worship services
2. The family gathers together to exchange gifts and prepare a special meal together
3. The day is shared with family and loved ones, focusing on His birth
    a. Families often prepare a birthday cake for Baby Jesus
    b. Time is spent taking food or other items to others less fortunate

VIII. Enjoy the study and remember that as time goes by, specifics and history can become a bit blurry, but the Reason for the season will always remain the same—Christ is born!

SHOW what you KNOW!

Check out these words from the **Lower Level** Spelling/Vocabulary List, and SHOW what you KNOW!

angel

peace

Lord

birth

glory

Jesus

stable

love

light

gold

inn

heaven

star

tax

sheep

sing

Spelling and Vocabulary
Lower Level

angel	lay
baby	light
birth	Lord
born	love
came	man
camel	oxen
child	pass
Christ	pay
city	peace
custom	people
day	Rome
donkey	room
east	rule
far	sang
fear	save
find	seek
flee	sheep
flock	sing
gifts	son
glory	sore
gold	stable
hay	star
heaven	tax
inn	tell
Jesus	temple
Jew	told
joy	warn
King	watch
lamb	wise
law	world

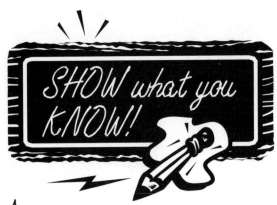

SHOW what you KNOW!

*Check out these words from the **Upper Level** Spelling/Vocabulary List, and SHOW what you KNOW!*

worship

Heaven

conceive

decree

nativity

foretold

advent

Bethlehem

lineage

manger

prophecy

shepherd

delivered

tidings

Christian

celebrate

Spelling and Vocabulary
Upper Level

abiding
accomplished
advent
afraid
angel
appear
behold
Bethlehem
birth
blessed

Caesar Augustus
carpenter
celebrate
Christian
Cleopatra
conceive
cousin
decree
delivered
donkey

Epiphany
father
favored
firstborn
flee
foretold
frankincense
fulfillment
Galilee
gold

Heaven
Herod
holiday
hymns
Israel
Jerusalem
Jew
John the Baptist
Joseph
journey

Judea
lineage
magi
manger
Mary
Messiah
mother
myrrh
nativity
Nazareth

proclamation
prophecy
Roman
Savior
shepherd
stable
swaddling
tidings
travel
worship

Now you have the chance to be a reporter. Interview a parent, grandparent, or neighbor. Ask questions about their favorite Christmas. Think ahead about the questions you will want to ask—the year of their favorite Christmas, what made it special, etc. Use the space below to report your findings. Happy Reporting!

The Very Best Christmas

Person Interviewed: _____

_____
_____
_____
_____
_____
_____
_____
_____
_____
_____
_____
_____
_____
_____
_____
_____
_____
_____
_____
_____
_____
_____
_____
_____

Writing Ideas

Here are some ideas to help incorporate writing in a unit study. Choose one or two and watch what happens!

1. One of the best ways to involve students in a Christmas unit study is to have them keep a Christmas journal. Have them record daily events, plans, preparations, special guests and holiday occasions. Their journals, prepared yearly, will provide a wonderful glimpse back in time for each student as the years go by, and will be enjoyed with their families in future years.

2. A fun writing project for the whole family can be the collection of interviews of each family member by the students. This can include both immediate family members as well as extended family members—siblings, aunts and uncles, grandparents, cousins, and on and on. Ask each person about his most memorable Christmas, the favorite gift that he made or gave for Christmas, his feelings about Christmas, favorite carol, etc. He might even have photographs to share, also. The students can compile the interviews, along with any photos or other information, to assemble into a family Christmas book. This can be added to with each passing Christmas.

3. Each student can write a letter to a friend, aging relative, invalid or pastor, thanking him for things he has done or memories he helped make, while sharing some of the student's thoughts on Christmas.

4. Remembering the excitement of the arrival of a new baby, have the children write or dictate a letter to Baby Jesus and His earthly parents, Mary and Joseph. In the letter, they can express their own excitement at His birth and words of comfort to the brand new family in the stable.

5. This time of year there is a rush to send Christmas cards to loved ones and family members. Try to get your children to write and create their own cards for their friends, sharing the good news of Christ's birth! I have a friend that does this every year, and saves one of the cards each year for their own decorations.

In the midst of celebrating the birth of Christ, we have a wonderful opportunity to share our blessings & the reason for the season with others. Use this space to plan some sharing & caring ideas for this holiday season.

People to Share With

Grocer

_____

Neighbor

_____

Mailman

_____

Pastor

_____

Bank Teller

_____

Friend

_____

Nursing Home

_____

Senior Citizen Center

_____

Sharing Ideas

Make Homemade Cookies   *Prepare A Meal*

Offer To Run An Errand   *Help With Decorations*

Help With Gift Wrapping   *Invite Over For Holiday*

Go Caroling   *Tell The Good News*

Tell That You Care

Activity Ideas

Activities provide a great way to reinforce the material that we learn in a unit study. They provide important hands-on learning, while we have fun and are challenged. As we work on a unit, we use items like those listed in the *Activity Resources,* as well as some of our own ideas to create some hands-on learning of our own. Here are a few activity ideas to get you started. Don't be surprised if the children come up with some great ones on their own!

1. With the birth of any new baby, the family often finds a special way to announce the birth to friends and neighbors. Have the children design their own special way to announce the birth of Jesus. Their creativity can really be encouraged here. Let them use household items, or come up with their own design using the computer and modern technology. As they are beginning to think about what they would like to design, work with them to help them determine who they are designing this for and what would they like to tell them. This should help focus their ideas. Some students might create a paper announcement, while others could develop their own video segment!

2. This special season when we celebrate His birth opens wide the door to our hearts, as well as our homes. Many times over the holidays we have unexpected or expected visitors, and it is fun to get the children to help prepare for these guests ahead of time. They can make a list of things to assemble in one place for "just-in-case" company—items like fresh linens, guest soap, a Bible, a few hand-made gifts, etc. You might also want to have them make a "Visitor's Book" or Guest Book that you will be able to keep for years to come. This will remind you of all the friends that have passed through your home.

3. This is a time of year that families work together to help others in need, sharing their time as well as their faith. Participate in some community help projects, if possible, particularly with the older children. A few places that usually welcome your help include the local children's home, homeless shelters, the Salvation Army, etc. Traditionally, area churches also work to help others in the community using special holiday projects.

Christmas MEMORIES

Use this area to record some special Christmas moments with family & friends.

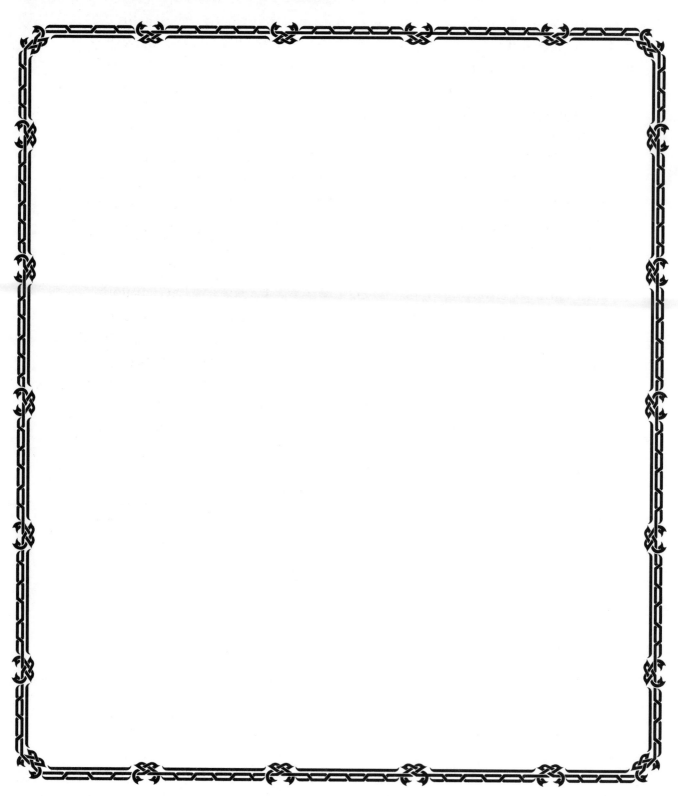

4. As a child, I grew up thinking that snow and Christmas were synonymous. I never really knew just what the climate and geography were like for that very First Christmas. Take the time to learn more about the Holy Land while working on this unit study. Have the students do some research on the food, plants, crops, weather, etc., for this special place. In doing so, they will be able to gain a better understanding of the place where Jesus spent His time while on Earth. To look at pictures or videos of the fields surrounding Bethlehem, the olive trees, the silhouette of the town in the evening, the shepherds that still tend their flocks there, one can develop a sense of what He saw and where He walked.

5. Christmas is a time when many families gather together to work on craft projects, planning and building things together. Whether it is making an afghan or quilt, building a footstool or tool box, these are some of the best times that you can all spend together, teaching important skills, making gifts as well as memories.

6. Work with the children on creating a Christmas Memories book, using a photo album or scrapbook. Collect photographs, church play programs, dried flowers and other memorabilia and organize it all in the album, labeling the years as you go. With each passing Christmas, have them add to the book. It becomes a fun tradition to take out the album over the holiday and reflect on all of the family's Christmas projects, guests and fun times that have been shared together.

Christmas MEMORIES

Use this area to record some special Christmas moments with family & friends.

Activity Resources

Activities provide a great way to reinforce the material that we learn in a unit study. They provide important hands-on learning, while we have fun and are challenged at the same time. There are numerous activity books available about the life of Christ, Christian Christmas crafts, etc., at many libraries, and your family will probably come up with some fun activities of their own. Here are some to consider:

Nativity Set, an easy-to-make woodworking project from **The Carpenter's Son Woodcraft**. This inexpensive kit allows you and your family to create your own heirloom Nativity scene. It comes with pre-cut figures and complete finishing directions. Older children (ages 10 and up) could complete this on their own, while younger children would need some help. While working on the set, consider reading aloud the book *The Christmas Miracle of Jonathan Toomey*, by Susan Wojciechowski (see the listing in Reading Resources). For ordering information, write to The Carpenter's Son Woodcraft, 3209 Willowbrook Circle, Waco, TX 76711, or call them at (817) 756-5261.

Nativity Scenes Paintables, a set of six different scenes of the Nativity, all printed on quality watercolor paper (includes brush and watercolor paints). Available from The Elijah Company, Rt. 2 Box 100-B, Crossville, TN 38555, or call them at (615) 456-6284.

Christian Holiday Arts and Crafts, by Rich and Sharon Jeffus. With holiday craft projects for both Thanksgiving and Christmas, this book has some simple and well-explained craft projects. Available from Visual Manna, P.O. Box 553, Salem, MO 65560, or call them at (314) 729-2100.

Keeping Christ in Christmas: Family Activities, Crafts, and Recipes, by Adell Harvey and Mari González. A lovely book full of simple ideas and inspiration for the entire family. Published by Abingdon Press, P.O. Box 801, Nashville, TN 37203. (800) 251-3320.

The Big Book of Great Gift Ideas, by Alice Chapin. This book has some wonderful ideas for simple low or no-cost gift ideas for Christians. Grades 6 - 12. Published by Tyndale House Publishers, Inc., Wheaton, IL

Christmas MEMORIES

Use this area to record some special Christmas moments with family & friends.

Get Ready, Celebrate, Rejoice: Inspiration and Activities for the Christmas Season, by Sue Kirk and Sally Wilke. Published by Standard Publishing, 8721 Hamilton Ave., Cincinnati, OH 45231. (800) 543-1353.

The Family Treasury of Great Holiday Ideas, A Barbour Book. From the cover: "Hundreds of ideas to help you make the most of the Thanksgiving and Christmas holidays, including contributions from today's most popular Christian authors." Published by Barbour and Company, Inc., P.O. Box 719, Uhrichsville, OH 44683. Available from Great Christian Books, P.O. Box 8000, Elkton, MD 21922-8000. (800) 775-5422.

Let's Draw the Nativity, by Anita Ganeri. Grades 3 - 8. Published by Random House, 400 Hahn Rd., Westminster, MD 21157. (800) 733-3000.

Holy Christmas rubber stamp set, from Personal Stamp Exchange and ***The First Noël*** rubber stamp set from Inkadinkado are fun to use with the children during this time of year. They provide just what you need to make your own family's Christmas cards. Available from Farm Country General Store, Rt. 1 Box 63, Metamora, IL 61548. (800) 551-FARM.

PROJECT Ideas

"And, lo, the angel of the Lord came upon them, and the glory of the Lord shone round about them: and they were sore afraid."
—Luke 2:9

Things to try, places to see, papers to write, books to read, things to make . . .

_____

_____

_____

_____

_____

_____

_____

_____

_____

_____

_____

_____

_____

_____

_____

_____

_____

_____

_____

_____

_____

Famous Art Resources

As you collect materials for this unit about Christmas and the birth of our Lord, you may want to consider studying masterpiece art works that focus on this Holy Season. Here are a few resources:

Special Topic Study Sets are available from University Prints to help teach various topics from an artistic viewpoint. The prints are high quality and very affordable. They measure 5.5" x 8". The topics sets to consider for this unit include:

Life of Christ in Art
Christmas Story in Art

Write for their brochure and further information:
>   University Prints
>   P.O. Box 485
>   Winchester, MA 01890

Rembrandt: Life of Christ . Grades 7 and up. A collection of some sketches and paintings where Rembrandt depicts various scenes from the life of Christ, combined with Scripture as text. Published by Thomas Nelson Publishers, P.O. Box 141000, Nashville, TN 37214. (800) 441-0511.

✓ **_Jesus of Nazareth: A Life of Christ Through Pictures_**. This book depicts the life of our Lord, using passages from the New Testament and masterpiece paintings from the National Gallery of Art in Washington. Published by Simon and Schuster Books for Children, 200 Old Tappan Rd., Old Tappan, NJ 07675. (800) 275-5755.

Carols for Christmas: From St. Patrick's Cathedral, arranged by John Dexter, Organist and Master of the Choristers, St. Patrick's Cathedral, Dublin. Published by Thomas Nelson Publishers, P.O. Box 141000, Nashville, TN 37214. (800) 441-0511. (Includes beautiful fine art from various museums, as well as a CD-ROM of the Christmas carols.)

Resources @HOME

"Behold, a virgin shall conceive, and bear a son, and shall call his name Immanuel."

—Isaiah 7:14

Tools, Books, Toys, Materials, Hobbies, Internet Sites…

Internet Resources

Here are some interesting sights on the Internet that you might want to visit while studying this unit. Please keep in mind that these pages, like all web pages, change from time to time. I recommend that you visit each sight first, before the children do, to view the content and make sure that it meets with your expectations. Also, use the **Subject Key Words** for search topics on Internet search engines, to find the latest additions that might pertain to this topic.

Visit Amanda Bennett's **Unit Study Web Page** for the latest updates on this unit study and the rest of the Unit Study Adventures Series:
http://www.unitstudy.com

Christian Christmas:

A Religious Christmas
http://www.execpc.com/~tmuth/st_john/xmas/main.htm

The Three Kings
http://www.members.carol.net/~asmsmsks/kings.htm

Christian Christmas Network - Advent Countdown
http://www.christcom.net/advent

The Christmas Experience
http://www.geocities.com/Heartland/Ranch/5775

The Season of Advent
http://www.geocities.com/Heartland/Ranch/5775/advent.html

The Christmas Story
http://www.geocities.com/Heartland/Ranch/5775/story.html

The Christian Calender
http://www.knight.org/advent/cathen/03158a.htm

The Legend of the Candy Cane
http://members.carol.net/~Easmsmsks/xristmas.htm

PLAN & Investigate

A contemplation of God's works, a generous concern for the good of mankind, and the unfeigned exercise of humility—these only, denominate men great and glorious.

—Addison

Plan your work, then work your plan!

_____
_____
_____
_____
_____
_____
_____
_____
_____
_____
_____
_____
_____
_____
_____
_____
_____
_____
_____
_____
_____
_____
_____
_____
_____

Christmas Music:

The Story of Silent Night
http://www.wilsonweb.com/archive/xmas/stille-n.htm

Christian Christmas Carols (Hymns)
http://www.hymnsite.com

Christmas Carol Singalong Page
http://jacks-shack.xtn.net/christmas/singalong.html

Christmas in History:

The Story of Saint Nicholas
http://members.carol.net/~asmsmsks/santa.htm

Christmas in Early America
http://christmas.com/html/early_america.html

Christmas Around the World:

Christmas in Many Languages
http://www.marskandiser.com/ChristmasLanguage.html

Christmas and New Year Traditions in the UK
http://www.rmplc.co.uk/eduweb/sites/wickham/xmas/xmastory.html

Christmas in the Carpathian Highlands
http://www.carpatho-rusyn.org/highland.htm

Christmas in Finland
http://virtual.finland.fi/finfo/english/joulueng.html#finnish father christmas

Christmas Around the World
http://www.soon.org.uk/country/christmas.htm

Ancient Rome:

Roman Art Gallery
http://fragments.gosite.com/roman.htm

The soul without imagination is what an observatory would be without a telescope.

—H.W. Beecher

The greatest events of an age are its best thoughts. It is the nature of thought to find its way into action.

—Bovee

Who?

What?

When?

Where?

Why?

Exploring Ancient World Cultures
http://eawc.evansville.edu/ropage.htm

Roman Art & Architecture
http://harpy.uccs.edu/roman/html/roman.html

Christmas Cooking:

Christmas Cookies Advent Calender
http://www.cookierecipe.com/cat/christmas.asp

Christmas Recipes
http://www.merry-christmas.com/recipes.htm

Ocean Spray
http://www.oceanspray.com

Butterball Turkey
http://www.butterball.com

Honeysuckle White Turkey
http://www.honeysucklewhite.com

Land O'Lakes
http://www.landolakes.com

Seasonal Solutions from Pillsbury
http://www.pillsbury.com/seasons

Miscellaneous:

The Gift of the Magi, by O. Henry (full text version of the classic)
http://www.auburn.edu/~vestmon/Gift_of_the_Magi.html

Chanukah
http://members.carol.net/~asmsmsks/chanukah.htm

Christmas Images
http://www.njwebworks.com/churchweb/gallery/christmas

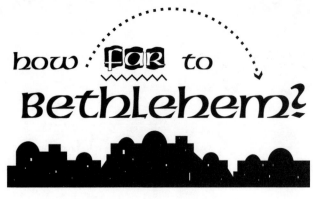

how far to Bethlehem?

How far is it from your town to Bethlehem? Use a world map to calculate the distance. Next use the space below to draw a map of the Holy Land and mark Nazareth and Bethlehem. How many miles did Joseph and Mary have to travel on their journey to Bethlehem?

N

Room Decorations

When working on a unit study, we try to decorate the room with items that relate to our current topic of interest. This allows the students to see the important information on a regular basis, and provides a place to view their own work. For Christmas, we tend to decorate not only our study, but the whole house! Consider some of the following ideas:

1. Over the years, we have accumulated quite a collection of handmade, unique or special Nativity scenes that we display all over the house. Letting each room have a special scene to remind us all of the real reason for the season is something we've come to enjoy over the years. The children have made their own sets for their rooms, and they help arrange the other scenes throughout the house.

2. With God's angels playing such an important role in sharing the Good News that night so long ago, we include them in our decorations. Let the children make their own angels, whether used as ornaments or as stand-alone decorations. There are numerous books in the library on Christmas crafts that have some fun ideas for making angels.

3. Consider having the children create posters of their idea of Bethlehem on the night of the Savior's birth. This might include the scene in the stable, the scene of the angels announcing the Birth to the shepherds, etc. They could use markers, scraps of material, construction paper, and anything else that happens to be on hand, making it more of a collage that you can display in your home.

4. Have the children draw a map of the Holy Land. They should label the towns and land features. Use poster board for the map, and have the children track Mary and Joseph on their journey from Nazareth to Bethlehem.

5. As you work on this unit, capture some of the children's thoughts and impressions on a "Christmas dinner tablecloth". Have them use fabric paint or indelible markers to decorate an inexpensive flat white twin sheet. They can draw pictures, write spelling words, draw maps or time lines—what a memory of fun times captured all in one place! Then, for Christmas dinner, have them save a spot on the cloth for the dinner menu, as well as a place for your guests to sign in. This will complete your Christmas unit study and create a tablecloth to be treasured for years to come.

Using resources that cover what life was like at the time of Jesus' birth, write a story describing what a day in the life of someone your age was like. Don't forget to include what they ate, learned, chores they might have had, etc. **Jesus and His Times** is one of several good reference books for this project.

A Day In The Life—At The Time Of Jesus' Birth

_____
_____
_____
_____
_____
_____
_____
_____
_____
_____
_____
_____
_____
_____
_____
_____
_____
_____

Sources: _____

_____

Videos

While learning about Christmas, there is usually an abundance of movies and other productions available on video tape. Many of these can be obtained through your local library or video store. Here are some suggestions for you!

Geography:

Try to locate some videos about Israel and its cities of both yesterday and today. There are many documentaries that have been made about the Holy Land. These are usually available through your church or library. One title that you might try to locate was produced by Focus on the Family, Colorado Springs, CO 80995 (800) 232-6459, and is titled **That The World May Know**. This will give the children and adults a balanced picture of the area and people where Christ was born, usually much different than the preconceived notions we get from Christmas cards!

Christ's Birth and Life:

One of our favorite videos for this topic is **The Greatest Story Ever Told**, a classic video about the life of Christ. There are several others available today, many of which will be enjoyed through the years by your family. Don't forget to see **Jesus of Nazareth**, from Gospel Films, if you get the chance. There is also a series of animated videos called **The Greatest Adventure Stories From the Bible**, produced by Hanna-Barbera. These are frequently found at Christian bookstores, and can be enjoyed by all ages. Some of our favorite titles when studying the birth and life of Christ include **The Nativity, The Miracles of Jesus** and **The Easter Story**.

Children's Christmas Videos:

1. **Electric Christmas**, from the Adventures in Odyssey Video Series, produced by Focus on the Family, Colorado Springs, CO 80995. (800) 232-6459.

2. **The Fight Before Christmas**, from the McGee and Me Video Series, produced by Focus on the Family, Colorado Springs, CO 80995. (800) 232-6459.

3. **A Christmas Story (Joy of Giving)**, from the Quigley's Village Video Series, produced by Zondervan, Order Processing, 5300 Patterson Ave., S.E. Grand Rapids, MI 49530. (800) 727-1309.

Our Christmas Traditions

Families around the world celebrate the birth of Christ with many different traditions. Some include a birthday party for Baby Jesus, attending a special midnight church service, helping those less fortunate, Christmas caroling, etc. What about your family? List and describe some of your traditions below.

Family Entertainment:

There are several Christmas classics on video now that can be enjoyed year after year. One of our favorites is **It's a Wonderful Life**, along with several other timeless movies, like **Hans Brinker**, or the **Silver Skates**, and **Little Women**.

CARING and SHARING

In the midst of celebrating the birth of Christ, we have a wonderful opportunity to share our blessings & the reason for the season with others. Use this space to plan some sharing & caring ideas for this holiday season.

People to Share With

Grocer _____

Neighbor _____

Mailman _____

Pastor _____

Bank Teller _____

Friend _____

Nursing Home _____

Senior Citizen Center _____

Sharing Ideas

Make Homemade Cookies

Offer To Run An Errand

Help With Gift Wrapping

Go Caroling

Tell That You Care

Prepare A Meal

Help With Decorations

Invite Over For Holiday

Tell The Good News

Field Trip Ideas

There are so many field trips that can be enjoyed while learning about Christ and Christmas, that it is hard to list all of the ones that you might want to consider. Here are some ideas to get you started!

1. In this season of so much community activity, try to locate a church production of a Living Nativity—a performance of the Nativity using live animals and real people. I'll never forget the time that our children participated in this type of production, and my youngest child was the infant child at a ripe old age of nine weeks! We will never forget how touching and meaningful the evening's ceremony was for the participants as well as those in the audience.

2. During this time of year, we try to focus on the true meaning of Christmas, the Birth of our Savior, and share the love and good news throughout our community. Often, there are churches that sponsor food drives for those in need during this season of love—consider participating in a drive with the whole family!

3. Attend the Christmas activities of your own church. These may include the hanging of the greens, the celebration of each Sunday of Advent, bell choir concerts, Christmas productions, and so on.

4. Take the children to see a local stage production of some of the Christmas classics, such as **The Nutcracker, The Gift of the Magi**, etc.

5. Nursing homes often welcome the chance to be on the receiving end of children's activities. Whether bringing decorations, clothing, or spending time to sing and share some happiness, the residents look forward to visits!

Famous PEOPLE of the TIME

There were many people involved in the events leading up to Christ's birth. Some, like the shepherds, remain nameless even though they played such memorable roles. Here are a few names that we do know. Choose one and see what kind of interesting information you can find out about this person.

_____
_____
_____
_____
_____
_____
_____
_____
_____
_____
_____
_____
_____
_____
_____
_____
_____
_____

Jesus
Mary
Joseph
John the Baptist
David

Augustus Caesar
Herod
Pontius Pilate
Elisabeth
Zacharias

Subject Word List

This list of **SUBJECT** search words has been included to help you with this unit study. To find material about Christmas, go to the card catalog or computerized holdings catalog in your library and look up:

Advent
Angels
Balthasar
Bethlehem
Caesar Augustus
Christian Faith
Christian Holidays
Christian Celebrations
Christmas Carols
Christmas History
Christmas Plays (drama)
Christmas
David (King)
Epiphany
Feast of the Nativity
Frankincense
Gaspar
Gospels
Herod
Israel
Jerusalem
Jesus Christ
John the Baptist
Joseph and Mary
Magi
Martin Luther
Melchoir
Myrrh
Nativity
Nazareth
St. Francis of Assisi

Investigate
an
EVENT

Select an event from the Sign of the Times timeline, and conduct your own investigation into the happening. Find out some of the details from some of your resource books, and summarize your findings.

_____

_____

_____

_____

_____

_____

_____

_____

_____

_____

_____

_____

_____

_____

_____

_____

_____

_____

_____

_____

_____

_____

_____

_____

_____

_____

_____

Trivia Questions

These questions have been included for fun and will reinforce some of the material that you might read during this study. Enjoy the search for answers, and then compare them with the answers we found located on pages 59 and 61.

1. What are frankincense and myrrh and where do they come from?

2. When the word "Magi" is used to describe the three wise men, what is meant and where might they have come from?

3. Why do some Christians celebrate Epiphany?

4. Who is believed to have written the words to the Christmas carol "Away in a Manger"?

5. Where did the idea for the simple nativity scene as a memorial to the Christ child, or creche, first originate?

6. What famous pastor of the Reformation is often credited with beginning the tradition of a candlelit tree to remind his church members of the starry heavens from which Christ came down?

7. Which state in the United States was the first to make Christmas a legal holiday?

8. What was the name of the father of John the Baptist?

Trivia Answers

1. What are frankincense and myrrh and where do they come from?

   Frankincense is a fragrant resin from the bark of East African and Arabian trees, burned as incense. Myrrh is a bitter-tasting dried sap from an African tree, also burned as incense, also from Arabian and African trees.

2. When the word "Magi" is used to describe the three wise men, what is meant and where might they have come from?

   "Magi" refers to an order of priests in Persia.

3. Why do some Christians celebrate Epiphany?

   Epiphany is the observation of Jesus' first appearance to Gentiles, the Wise Men (Magi).

4. Who is believed to have written the words to the Christmas carol "Away in a Manger"?

   Martin Luther is often given credit for the words of this carol, which was originally written in German

5. Where did the idea for the simple nativity scene as a memorial to the Christ child, or creche, first originate?

   St. Francis of Assisi inspired this in an attempt to refocus Christians on the birth of Christ, as part of the religious revival that he led.

6. What famous pastor of the Reformation is often credited with beginning the tradition of a candlelit tree to remind his church members of the starry heavens from which Christ came down?

   Martin Luther

7. Which state in the United States was the first to make Christmas a legal holiday?

   Alabama, in 1836

8. What was the name of the father of John the Baptist?

   Zacharias

Reference Resources
History

While the books listed below are rich in history, don't overlook the best history reference—the Bible!

✓ **Jesus and His Times**, from the editors of Readers' Digest. Published by Readers' Digest Association, Inc., Customer Relations, Pleasantville, NY. (800) 234-9000. An excellent resource for a study of the Hebrew world that Jesus was born in, with colorful photographs and maps, along with well-researched text.

✓ **Augustus Caesar's World: 44 B.C. to 14 A.D.**, by Genevieve Foster. Grades 5 - 12. Originally published in 1947 by Charles Scribner's Sons. Reading like a novel, this book provides a wealth of background on the world of the Romans during the era of our Lord's birth, as well as interesting insight into people that were in power at the time of Augustus Caesar (Herod, Cleopatra, Mark Antony). Available from The Back Pack, P.O. Box 125, Ernul, NC 28527. (919) 244-0728.

The Jews in the Time of Jesus, by Peter Connolly. Grades 5 - 12. Published by Oxford University Press, 2001 Evans Rd., Cary, NC 27513. (800) 451-7556.

In Jesus' Time: Teaching Bible History to Children of All Ages, by Kathryn Merrill and Kristy Christian. Published by Rainbow Books, P.O. Box 430, Highland City, FL 33846. (813) 648-4420. A study guide that helps introduce Jesus' life and times to students.

Children's Atlas of the Bible, by Nicola Baxter. Grades 3 - 8. Published by Smithmark Publishers, U.S. Media Group, Rariton Plaza 3, Edison, NJ 08337. (800) 932-0070. Available from Great Christian Books, P.O. Box 8000, Elkton, MD 21922-8000. (800) 775-5422.

Baker's Bible Atlas, by Charles E. Pfeiffer. Grades 5 - 12. Published by Baker Book House, P.O. Box 6287, Grand Rapids, MI 49516. (800) 877-2665.

CHRISTMAS
AROUND THE WORLD

Choose a foreign country and investigate their traditional Christmas celebrations. How do they celebrate, what do they eat, when do they begin their celebration, etc. Summarize your findings below. Locate the country on a world map too!

✓ **The Readers' Digest Book of Christmas**, Grades 7 - 12. Published by Readers' Digest Association, Inc., Customer Relations, Pleasantville, NY. (800) 234-9000. Opens with the Nativity and some beautiful fine art illustrations, includes chapters on Christmas and its history, literature of Christmas and celebration of Christmas around the world.

✓ **Christmas and Its Customs**, by Christina Hole. Grades 7 and up. An older book (copyright 1957), with interesting historical information on Christmas and traditions in Europe. Published by M. Barrows and Company, New York, NY.

✓ **Bible Lands (Eyewitness Books Series),** by Jonathan N. Tubb. Published by Knopf, Subsidiary of Random House, 400 Hahn Rd., Westminster, MD 21157. (800) 733-3000.

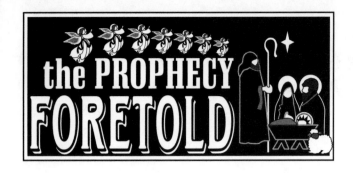

the PROPHECY FORETOLD

In the Old Testament of the Bible, the birth of Christ is foretold in many different Scriptures. Use this space to find and list several of these passages, as well as the New Testament Scriptures that fulfill each prophecy about the Christ Child.

"For unto us a child is born, unto us a Son is given: and the government shall be upon His shoulder: and His name shall be called Wonderful, Counsellor, The mighty God, The everlasting Father, The Prince of Peace."

—Isaiah 9:6

Reference Resources
The Nativity

The Story of Christmas, retold by Linda Jennings. Grades PreK - 4. Published by Ladybird Books, Inc., Auburn, Maine 04210.

The Story of the Nativity, by Elizabeth Winthrop. Grades K - 6. Published by Simon & Schuster Books for Young Readers, 200 Old Tappan Rd., Old Tappan, NJ 07675. (800) 275-5755.

Jesus Comes: the Story of Jesus' Birth for Children, by Lyn and Ron Klug. Grades 3 - 8. Published by Augsburg Fortress Publications, 426 South Fifth Street, P.O. Box 1209, Minneapolis, MN 55440-1209. (800) 323-4648.

The Nativity: A Bible Story Pop-up Book, by Sue E. Brown. Grades PreK - 3. Published by Thomas Nelson Publishers, P.O. Box 14100, Nashville, TN 37214. (800) 441-0511.

The First Christmas: Luke 2: 1-20: The Birth of Jesus, by Mary M. Simon. (Hear Me Read Series). Grades 1 -3. Published by Concordia Publishing House, 3558 Jefferson Ave., St. Louis, MO 63118. (800) 325-3040.

The Birth of Jesus, by Rosalind Sutton. (Now You Can Read Stories From the Bible Series). Grades PreK - 5. Published by Thomas Nelson Publishers, P.O. Box 141000, Nashville, TN 37214. (800) 441-0511.

Two From Galilee, Love Story of Mary and Joseph and **Three From Galilee, the Young Man From Nazareth**, both by Marjorie Holmes. Published by Fleming H. Revell, owned by Baker Book House, P.O. Box 6287, Grand Rapids, MI 49516. (800) 877-2665.

All Paths Lead to Bethlehem, by Patricia and Fredrick McKissack. Grades PreK - 3. Published by Augsburg Fortress Publications, 426 South Fifth Street, P.O. Box 1209, Minneapolis, MN 55440-1209. (800) 328-4648.

Tomorrow We Go to Bethlehem, by John Metavish. Published by Abingdon Press, P.O. Box 801, Nashville, TN 37202. (800) 251-3320.

Gifts of the WISE MEN

The wise men brought gifts to honor Jesus. Use the space below to list the gifts and write a definition of each one.

"Now when Jesus was born in Bethlehem of Judaea in the days of Herod the king, behold, there came wise men from the east to Jerusalem."
"Saying, Where is he that is born King of the Jews? for we have seen his star in the east and are come to worship him."

—Matthew 2:1-2

The Birth of God: Recovering the Mystery of Christmas, by John B. Rogers. Published by Abingdon Press, P.O. Box 801, Nashville, TN 37202. (800) 251-3320.

✓ **Brother Francis and the Friendly Beasts**, by Margaret Hodges. Grades 2 - 5. Published by Atheneum Books for Young Readers, a Division of Simon and Schuster, 200 Old Tappan Rd., Old Tappan, NJ 07675. (800) 223-2336.

Use this page to develop a family plan for celebrating Christ's birth this year. Enjoy making the plans, and remember to stay flexible!

How shall we celebrate? _____

_____
_____
_____
_____
_____
_____
_____
_____

Who shall we invite to join in our celebration? _____

_____
_____
_____
_____
_____
_____
_____
_____
_____

What shall we do to prepare? _____

_____
_____
_____
_____
_____
_____
_____
_____
_____

Reference Resources
Family Celebration

Before and After Christmas, by Debbie O'Neal. Published by Augsburg Fortress Publications, 426 South Fifth Street, P.O. Box 1209, Minneapolis, MN 55440-1209. (800) 328-4648.

The Big Book of Great Gift Ideas, by Alice Chapin. Published by Tyndale House Publishers, Inc., Wheaton, IL

The Family Treasury of Great Holiday Ideas, A Barbour Book. Published by Barbour and Company, Inc., P.O. Box 719, Uhrichsville, OH 44683.

Come, Lord Jesus: Devotions for the Home Advent/Christmas/Epiphany, by Susan Briehl. Published by Augsburg Fortress Publications, 426 South Fifth Street, P.O. Box 1209, Minneapolis, MN 55440-1209. (800) 328-4648.

The Jesse Tree, by Raymond and Georgene Anderson. Published by Augsburg Fortress Publications, 426 South Fifth Street, P.O. Box 1209, Minneapolis, MN 55440-1209. (800) 328-4648.

Christ in Christmas: A Family Advent Celebration, by James M. Boice. Published by NavPress Publishing Group, P.O. Box 9099, Oxnard, CA 93031. (800) 366-7788.

Keeping Christ in Christmas: Family Activities, Crafts and Recipes, by Adell Harvey and Marie Gonzalez. Published by Abingdon Press, P.O. Box 801, Nashville, TN 37202. (800) 251-3320.

Unplug the Christmas Machine: How to Really Participate in the Joys of Christmas, by Jo Robinson and Jean Staehel. Published by Quill, a Division of Morrow & Company, attn: Order Dept., 39 Plymouth St., Fairfield, NJ 07004. (800) 843-9389.

PROJECT Ideas

Things to try, places to see, papers to write, books to read, things to make . . .

Get Ready, Celebrate, Rejoice: Inspiration and Activities for the Christmas Season, by Sue Kirk and Sally Wilke. Published by Standard Publishing, 8121 Hamilton Ave., Cincinnati, OH 45231. (800) 543-1353.

The Christmas Book, by Alice Slaikeu Lawhead. For Moms who need inspiration as well as organization during a busy holiday season, while keeping your focus on Christ! Published by Crossway Books, a Division of Good News Publishers, 1300 Crescent St., Wheaton, IL 60187. (800) 635-7993.

Jesus Tree, by Annette Dellinger. Grades Pre K–2. Published by Concordia Publishing House, 3558 S. Jefferson Ave., St. Louis, MO 63118. (314) 268-1000.

Advent Arts and Christmas Crafts, by Jeanne Heiberg. Published by Paulist Press, 997 MacArthur Blvd., Mahwah, NJ 07430. (201) 825-7300.

Through the years since Christ's birth, many beautiful hymns have been written in honor of His birth. Some of these are listed below, and there are many others. Use the Internet Website hymnsite.com to find the lyrics and hear these, and many other hymns.

Choose one of your favorite Christmas carols and investigate the history of the song—who wrote the music, who wrote the lyrics, and how it came about!

Away In a Manger
O Little Town of Bethlehem
Joy to the World
Angels We Have Heard on High
Silent Night, Holy Night

Hark! The Herald Angels Sing
O Holy Night
What Child is This?
The First Noël

Reference Resources
Art and Music

And The Angels Sing: A Song Book of Christmas Carols, music arranged by Andrew Davis. Published by Baker Book House, P.O. Box 6287, Grand Rapids, MI 49516. (800) 877-2665.

My Favorite Christmas Carols, pictures by Kathy Wilburn. Grades 2 - 6. Published by HarperCollins Children's Books, 1000 Keystone Industrial Park, Scranton, PA 18512. (800) 242-7737.

Christmas Carols & Their Stories, by Christopher Idle. Published by Chariot/Victor, owners of Lion Publishing, 4050 Lee Vance View, Colorado Springs, CO 80918. (800) 437-4337.

Rembrandt: Life of Christ, Grades 7 and up. A collection of some sketches and paintings where Rembrandt depicts various scenes from the life of Christ, combined with Scripture as text. Published by Thomas Nelson Publishers, P.O. Box 1410000, Nashville, TN 37214. (800) 441-0511.

Jesus of Nazareth: A Life of Christ Through Pictures, This book depicts the life of our Lord, using passages from the New Testament and masterpiece paintings from the National Gallery of Art in Washington. Published by Simon and Schuster Books for Children, 200 Old Tappan Rd., Old Tappan, NJ 07675. (800) 275-5755.

Carols for Christmas: From St. Patrick's Cathedral, arranged by John Dexter, Organist and Master of the Choristers, St. Patrick's Cathedral, Dublin. Published by Thomas Nelson Publishers, Nashville, TN.

George Frideric Handel: Composer of Messiah, by Charles Ludwig. (Sower Series) Grades 5 and up. Published by Mott Media, 1000 E. Huron, Milford, MI 48381. (800) 421-6645.

Handel, by Ann Rachlin. (Famous Children Series). Grades 3 and up. Published by Barron's Childrens, 250 Wireless Blvd., Hauppauge, NY 11788. (800) 645-3476.

Silent Night: The Song and Its Story, by Margaret Hodges. Published by Wm. B. Eerdmans Publishing Co., 255 Jefferson, S.E., Grand Rapids, MI 49503. (800) 253-7521.

The soul without imagination is what an observatory would be without a telescope.

—H.W. Beecher

The greatest events of an age are its best thoughts. It is the nature of thought to find its way into action.

—Bovee

Who? _____

What? _____

When? _____

Where? _____

Why? _____

Reference Resources
Miscellaneous

✓ ***The Pioneer Lady's Country Christmas: A Gift of Old-fashioned Recipes and Memories of Christmas Past***, by Jane Watson Hopping. Published by Villard Books, a Division of Random House, 400 Hahn Rd., Westminster, MD 21157. (800) 733-3000.

✓ ***My Christmas Treasury***, by Norman Vincent Peale. Grades 9 and up. Published by HarperCollins Publishers, 1000 Keystone Industrial Park, Scranton, PA 18512. (800) 242-7737.

Let's Draw the Nativity, by Anita Ganeri. Grades 3 - 8. Published by Random House, 400 Hahn Rd., Westminster, MD 21157. (800) 733-3000.

Kids Create! Christmas with Clay: Creating Your Own Ornaments and Bring Home the Meaning of Christmas, from Tyndale for Kids. Grades 2 - 5. Published by Tyndale House Publishers, Wheaton, IL.

Christmas Blessings, by Helen Steiner Rice. Published by Baker Book House, P.O. Box 6287, Grand Rapids, MI 49516-6287. (800) 877-2665.

Let's Keep Christmas, by Peter Marshall. Published by Chosen Books, P.O. Box 6287, Grand Rapids, MI 49516-6287. (800) 877-2665.

Christian Holiday Arts and Crafts, by Rich and Sharon Jeffus. Published by Visual Manna, P.O. Box 553, Salem MO 65560. (314) 729-2100.

✓ ***Cleopatra***, by Diane Stanley and Peter Vennema. Grades 2 - 6. Published by William Morrow and Company, 39 Plymouth St., Fairfield, NJ 07004. (800) 843-9389.

Favorite Christmas BOOKS

Of the many books written about Jesus' birth and Chrismas, most families have a favorite title or two. At our house, we place our favorite Christmas books in a large wicker basket in the family room right after Thanksgiving. They are picked up and read many times during the holiday season. Some of our favorites include Jesus' Christmas Party *by Nicholas Allan,* The Christmas Miracle of Jonathan Toomey *by Susan Wojciechowski, and many others.*

What about your family? List some of your favorite Christmas books below.

Reading Resources

Jesus' Christmas Party, by Nicholas Allan. Grades PreK-2. Published by Doubleday Books, 1540 Broadway, New York, NY 10036. (800) 323-9872.

A Penny for a Hundred, by Mary Beth Owens. Grades 4-8. Published by Down East Books, P.O. Box 679, Camden, ME 04843. (800) 766-1670.

The Beasts of Bethlehem, by X.J. Kennedy. Grades 2 and up. Published by Margaret McElderry, imprint of Simon & Schuster Children's, 200 Old Tappan Road, Old Tappan, NJ 07675. (800) 223-2336.

Brother Francis and the Friendly Beasts, by Margaret Hodges. Grades PreK-2. Published by Atheneum, imprint of Simon & Schuster Children's, 200 Old Tappan Road, Old Tappan, NJ 07675. (800) 223-2336.

Bethlehem's Busy: What's Going On?, by Muff Singer and Lynn Adams. Grades PreK-2. Published by Standard Publishing, 8121 Hamilton Avenue, Cincinnati, OH 45231. (800) 543-1301.

A New Coat For Anna, by Harriet Ziefert and Anita Lobel. Grades K - 3. Published by Scholastic, Inc., P.O. Box 7502, Jefferson City, MO 65102. (800) 325-6149.

Merry Birthday, Nora Noël, by Ann Dixon. Grades PreK - 2. Published by Eerdmans Publishing Company, 255 Jefferson SE, Grand Rapids, MI 49503. (800) 253-7521.

The Christmas Strangers, by Marjorie Thayer. Grades 3- 6. Published by Children's Press, P.O. Box 1331, Danbury, CT 06813. (800) 621-1115.

The Christmas Miracle of Jonathan Toomey, by Susan Wojciechowski. Grades 1 - 6. Published by Candlewick Press, 2067 Massachusetts Avenue, Cambridge, MA 02140.

One Wintry Night, by Ruth Bell Graham. Grades 3 - 7. Published by Baker Book House, P.O. Box 6287, Grand Rapids, MI 49516. (800) 877-2665.

The Animals' Gift, by Szabolcs de Vajay. Grades K - 3. Published by Simon & Schuster Books for Young Readers, 200 Old Tappan Rd., Old Tappan, NJ 07675. (800) 223-2348.

"Thou wilt shew me the path of life; in thy presence is fullness of joy; at thy right hand there are pleasures for evermore."

—Plalm 16:11

List some questions for which you would like to research the answers.

_____

_____

_____

_____

_____

_____

_____

_____

_____

_____

_____

_____

_____

_____

_____

_____

_____

_____

_____

_____

_____

_____

_____

The Crippled Lamb, by Max Lucado with Jenna, Andrea and Sarah Lucado. Grades PreK - 4. Published by Word Kids!, Word Publishing, Dallas, TX.

The Tale of Three Trees: A Traditional Folktale, retold by Angela Elwell Hunt. Grades PreK - 8. Published by Chariot/Victor, owners of Lion Publishing, 4050 Lee Vance View, Colorado Springs, CO 80918. (800) 437-4337.

A Little House Christmas: Holiday Stories From the Little House Books, by Laura Ingalls Wilder. Grades 3 - 7. Published by HarperCollins Children's Books, 1000 Keystone Industrial Park, Scranton, PA 18512. (800) 242-7737.

Gutenberg's Gift: A Book Lover's Pop-Up Book, by Nancy Willard. Grades PreK and up. A fascinating pop-up book for all ages, presents a fictionalized account of Gutenberg's life, focusing on his work to complete his first printed Bible for a Christmas gift for his wife. Published by Harcourt Brace Jovanovich, 6277 Sea Harbor Dr., Orlando, FL 32886. (800) 782-4479.

Working Outline

I.   Introduction

    A.   Reason for the holiday, the birth of our Lord!

        1.   With His birth came the light of the world, the promise of our future

        2.   God became man on that night so long ago, in the form of a helpless tiny infant

    B.   Impact of the holiday on times of yesterday and today

        1.   Christians celebrate His birth with worship and praise

        2.   Much of the world stops and rests, taking notice of Christians and their faith

        3.   Even our days are measured by His birth, as our calendar (Gregorian) is based on time *"anno Domini"* (A.D.) since His coming

    C.   Many lessons to be learned through the study of this holiday and Christ's birth

1. Strengthens our faith by making us aware of God's power and plan, seeing His timing and love throughout history

2. Introduces us to history at that special time in civilization, the spread of power, the development of kingdoms, and particularly the eventual spread of Christianity

3. Provides a wonderful opportunity to learn more about the Jews, the earthly race that God chose for His Son—their faith and their lives at the time of His birth

II. Life in the time of Jesus' birth

A. Government of Judea, a Roman province

1. Herod, King of Judea at Christ's birth, was put into power by the Roman government

   a. In the year 40 B.C., Herod was driven from Palestine by Parthians seeking to control Judea

   b. Fleeing, he journeyed to Egypt, seeking help to get to Rome for assistance

      (1) Cleopatra, seeing his military abilities, offered Herod a command in her army

(2) Refusing her offer, Herod continued on to Rome with Cleopatra's assistance and a personal referral to Mark Antony

c. Arriving in Rome, Herod sought help from Mark Antony, an old family friend

(1) Antony, seeing the value of Herod in Palestine, appeared before the Senate to recommend that Herod be made King

(2) The Senate agreed with Antony and passed a decree that made Herod the King of Judea

(3) Accompanied by both Antony and Octavian (soon to be Caesar Augustus), Herod was given his new title. He was also given troops to go back and claim Jerusalem for Rome

(4) In the 37 B.C., Herod and his Roman soldiers successfully attacked Jerusalem and took over control of Palestine for Rome

2. Herod, a tyrant ruler

a. Herod was half Jew (not by ancestry, but by conversion) and half Arab, and was very much hated by the Jews of Judea

b. It is said that Herod was often controlled by demons, tortured and paranoid for most of his time as a ruler

c. Herod was known to be merciless, killing his own wife, children, family members and many others

d. Herod ruled Palestine for approximately 33 years (37 BC to 4 BC)

B. Daily life of the Israelites

1. Family life

a. Life revolved around the family

b. The husband was the family leader, both spiritually and legally

c. The husband was also the provider for his wife and children, and early religious educator, as well

d. The wife was responsible for the home, cleaning the home, watching the children, making clothing, bringing water from the well and preparing food

e.   The families observed the Sabbath as a day of rest and worship, as well as keeping other holy days

2.   Education and religion

    a.   To Jews, education and religion went hand in hand, and were woven throughout their daily lives

    b.   Children were taught at an early age about their religion, through observation on the Sabbath, as well as instruction at home

    c.   Boys, at the age of five, began school, attending six days a week, usually at the synagogue

3.   Economic life

    a.   Villages had farmers as well as tradesmen among their residents

    b.   The tradesmen included carpenters, weavers, leather crafters and blacksmiths

    c.   Trade in the village usually involved bartering services for food and other items

C. Religion

    1. The Jewish faith was a focal point in their lives; everything revolved around their faith and its applications to daily life

    2. The Jews were the chosen people of God

    3. Persecuted, overthrown and ruled over, they awaited the arrival of a King who had been promised for hundreds and hundreds of years

    4. The Torah was the record of their faith and its meaning, while the synagogue was their central place of worship

D. The Roman Empire

    1. At the time of Jesus' birth, Caesar Augustus was the first emperor of Rome

    2. The Empire consisted of the countries around the Mediterranean Sea, including Egypt, Judea, Greece, Macedonia, Italy, France (Gaul) and Spain

    3. The most powerful empire on earth at that time, Rome controlled vast territories and many people of numerous nationalities

4. The Romans built roads, improved trade routes and developed many other technological advances in their time

5. Trade included items such as cloth, spices, olive oil, precious metals, glass, lumber, wine and grain

III. Preparing for the birth of Christ in Israel

A. The Israelites had been waiting for centuries for the promised Savior

B. They had studied and learned the prophecies of His birth (quoted here from the Old Testament of the King James Version (KJV) of the Bible)

1. His birth is promised: "For unto us a child is born, unto us a son is given: and the government shall be upon his shoulder: and his name shall be called Wonderful, Counsellor, The mighty God, The everlasting Father, The Prince of Peace." Isaiah 9:6

2. He would be born of a virgin: "Therefore the Lord himself shall give you a sign; Behold, a virgin shall conceive, and bear a son, and shall call his name Immanuel." Isaiah 7:14

3. He would be from the tribe of Judah: "The sceptre shall not depart from Judah, nor a lawgiver from between his feet, until Shiloh come; and unto him shall the gathering of the people be." Genesis 49:10

4. He would be born in Bethlehem: "But thou, Bethlehem Ephratah, though thou be little among the thousands of Judah, yet out of thee shall he come forth unto me that is to be ruler of Israel; whose goings forth have been from of old, from everlasting." Micah 5:2

5. He would be worshipped by the Magi: "Thus saith the Lord, the Redeemer of Israel, and his Holy One, to him whom man despiseth, to him whom the nation abhorreth, to a servant of rulers, Kings shall see and arise, princes also shall worship…" Isaiah 49:7

6. The Magi shall bring gifts: "The multitude of camels shall cover thee, the dromedaries of Midian and Ephah; all they from Sheba shall come: they shall bring gold and incense; and they shall shew forth the praises of the Lord." Isaiah 60:6

C. They probably expected a king; one that was physically powerful and could demolish the Romans and other tyrants and save them from their misery

D. They were not expecting a tiny helpless baby, born almost unnoticed, heralded only by angels and shepherds from the fields

IV. The Birth of Jesus Christ, Son of God

A. The announcement of the upcoming birth of John the Baptist

1. Zacharias is visited by the angel Gabriel, telling him of the son that he and Elisabeth would soon have

2. Elisabeth, Mary's cousin, conceives, in her advanced years

3. John the Baptist is born, a few months before Jesus, growing to serve God and prepare the way for Jesus' ministry

B. The announcement of the upcoming birth of Jesus to Mary

1. The angel Gabriel also visited Mary, in the city of Nazareth, when Elisabeth was six months pregnant

   a. Gabriel told Mary that God had found favor with her, and that she would conceive the Son of God and that His name would be Jesus

   b. The angel also told Mary the news of Elisabeth's pregnancy

   c. Mary accepted the angel's news, saying "..be it unto me according to thy word." (Luke 1:38)

2. Mary went to visit Elisabeth, sharing the news from the angel

C. The announcement of the birth to Joseph

1. Joseph, learning of Mary's pregnancy, considered putting her away privately to avoid making her a public example

2. In a dream, the angel of the Lord reassured Joseph about Mary and the baby

    a. The angel instructed Joseph to go ahead and take Mary as his wife

    b. The angel explained that Mary's baby was conceived of the Holy Spirit, and was to be called Jesus, and that He would save His people from their sins

3. Arising from his dream, Joseph did as the angel instructed, taking Mary as his wife

D. Joseph and Mary travel from their home in Nazareth to Bethlehem

1. A decree was sent out from Caesar Augustus, stating that all the world should be taxed, having everyone return to the town of their birth to enroll for the tax

2. Born in Bethlehem, Joseph took Mary and travelled with her to the place of his birth

a. The journey covered approximately 90 miles, which was a long trip in those days (about a five-day walk), especially with a woman in such a late stage of pregnancy

b. One of the prophecies that they had learned as children stated that the King would be from Bethlehem; this thought must have both excited them as well as scared them a bit as they made their way back to Bethlehem

c. Bethlehem was located on a low rocky ridge just south of Jerusalem, surrounded by olive groves and fertile fields

E. After arriving in Bethlehem, they found that there was no room for them in the inn (also known as a caravansary—a resting place for caravans of travelers)

1. In the time of enrollment, there were probably crowds of people in the town, making it difficult to find a room for them to stay in during their visit

2. They probably stayed in a stable or a cave on the outskirts of town, where animals were oftentimes kept in the evening

F. While in Bethlehem, the days were accomplished that Mary should deliver her firstborn Son!

1. Jesus was born there in Bethlehem, wrapped in swaddling clothes and laid in a manger

a. Swaddling clothes were usually made by the mother-to-be for her new baby, and were used to bind the newborn baby's limbs

b. A manger was the word used to refer to an animal feed trough, usually made of wood or carved into the wall of a cave

2. With His birth, Jesus fulfilled the prophecies of old, being born of a virgin in Bethlehem, from the line of David

G. Meanwhile, out in the fields surrounding Bethlehem, an angel of the Lord appeared to shepherds that were guarding their flocks through the night

1. The angel explained to them that the Savior had been born that day, in the city of David (Bethlehem)

2. The angel also told them that they would find the baby wrapped in swaddling clothes, lying in a manger

3. Afraid of the angel at first, the shepherds heard the words in awe

4.   After telling the shepherds of the news of Jesus' birth, the angel was joined by a multitude of angels that were praising God, saying "Glory to God in the highest, and on earth peace, good will toward men." (Luke 2:14)

5.   After the angels were gone, the shepherds decided to go into Bethlehem to find this baby

6.   Hastening to Bethlehem, the shepherds found the baby lying in a manger

7.   After finding the babe, they departed, glorifying and praising God for all that they had seen

V.   Jesus is presented to the world

A.   Mary and Joseph travelled with baby Jesus to the temple of Jerusalem, when He was approximately 40 days old, in accordance with Jewish laws

     1.   Mary's period of separation after the birth of the baby was over and they travelled to Jerusalem for the rites of purification

     2.   Baby Jesus was presented for redemption before God, remembering His protection of Israel's firstborn sons as they fled Egypt

B.   While at the temple, they were met by a man named Simeon

    1.   Simeon had been assured by the Holy Ghost that he would not die until he had seen Jesus, and he recognized the Savior, as Joseph and Mary entered the temple

    2.   Taking Jesus in his arms and blessing God, Simeon said of Jesus, "A light to lighten the Gentiles, and the glory of thy people Israel." (Luke 2:32)

C.   Also at the temple was Anna, a prophetess of great age

    1.   She had prayed and fasted for years at the temple

    2.   She, too, recognized the Savior as they were in the temple, and thanked God for Him

    3.   Anna then shared the news of the Savior with others who visited the temple for redemption

D.   Some time in the first two years of His life, Jesus was visited by wise men from the East

    1.   They had followed a bright star to Jerusalem, and were asking the whereabouts of the King of the Jews

2. Their questions got the attention of Herod, who considered himself to be King of the Jews

    a. Herod brought the wise men to meet with him privately, and asked questions about their knowledge of this King

    b. After inquiring of his scribes and priests as to the location of where the "Christ" would be born, Herod sent the wise men to Bethlehem, asking them to return and tell him where the baby was so that he, too, could go and worship the King

3. The wise men journeyed on to Bethlehem, following the bright star as it went before them, and brought them to the young child, Jesus

    a. They fell down and worshipped Him

    b. They presented him with treasures fit for a king (gold, frankincense and myrrh)

    c. Being warned in a dream to not return to Herod, the wise men left for their country another way

4. Herod, after determining that he had been tricked by the Wise Men, ordered that all children under two years old were to be killed

5.   Joseph took Mary and Jesus and fled to Egypt, after being warned in dream about Herod's plan to have the child destroyed

VI.   History of the holiday

A.   Early Christians

    1.   Evidence of the earliest celebration of the Nativity was found in paintings on the walls of the catacombs, where early Christians worshiped in safety

    2.   As Paul and others spread the Christian faith, the churches became established, and Romans were converted to Christianity

    3.   By 135 A.D., Christians began to assemble to sing the angels' hymns on the Holy Night of the Nativity

    4.   In the year 312 A.D., Emperor Constantine made Christianity the religion of Rome

B.   The early Church

    1.   The Church, trying to draw in more people to Christianity and away from the worship of false gods, made an effort to identify various Christian holidays

2. The Church established the Feast of the Nativity, or celebration of Christ's birth, on December 25th

    a. The church frequently timed Christian holidays to coincide with the pagan festivities, to help the people make an easier transition to Christianity

    b. Pope Julius I (337 - 352 A.D.), in an effort to honor the birth of Jesus, had extensive research performed to try to establish the date of His birth

    c. Prior to this time, Christmas had been celebrated with Epiphany on January 6

    d. There are many different explanations of the choice of December 25th as the date of Christmas, varying from pagan roots to tax records of Rome, etc.

3. With his own conversion to Christianity, Emperor Theodosius I, in 374 A.D., outlawed all pagan festivities, including the Olympics as well as the celebration of Saturnalia and other pagan festivities that occurred at the end of the year

C. The Middle Ages

1. With the spread of Christianity throughout Europe, so went the celebration of Christmas and other Christian observances

2. Depending on the government or ruler of the time, the celebration of Christmas waxed and waned from times of religious worship and praise to times of eating and wild festivities

D. The Reformation

1. King Henry VIII formed a new church, the Church of England, breaking away from the Roman Catholic Church

2. With the Reformation came great changes in the church, helped along by famous figures such as Martin Luther, John Knox, etc., forming the foundation of the Protestant church

3. The Puritans and Separatists refused to worship according to the dictates of King Henry VIII and the leaders that followed him; they did not celebrate Christmas, as it was looked upon as having associations with the rituals and traditions of the King's Church as well as having its roots in pagan festivities

E. Colonization of America

1. This defiance towards celebrating Christmas was brought to America by the Puritans and Separatists

2. In the early years of colonization, it was actually against the law to celebrate Christmas in some parts of this country

3.	As more and more people from other parts of Europe came to settle in the United States, they brought their own special Christian celebrations of Christmas with them

F.	Christmas becomes a holiday in America

   1.	In 1836, Alabama was the first state to declare Christmas a legal holiday, soon to be followed by all of the other states

   2.	Celebrated in many ways throughout the country, Christmas has become a favorite holiday across the nation

   3.	Like any other holiday or political idea or human effort, Christmas can be viewed from many perspectives

      a.	Some choose to celebrate the holiday to observe the real reason for the season, the birth of our Lord

      b.	Others choose to celebrate the season for both religious reasons, as well as observing other family traditions

      c.	In this materialistic world that we live in, some choose to celebrate the holiday just for a day off from work, a time of gathering family together and a time of revelry

VII. The Christian celebration of Christmas includes many different traditions and events, with the central theme being the birth of Christ

A. Advent is a holy time of the seasons that some celebrate, a time of fasting and prayer, preparing hearts for the coming of the King

　　1. Advent begins on the fourth Sunday before Christmas

　　2. The days of Advent are marked with special daily devotions, weekly services and calendars

B. Some families celebrate the twelve days of Christmas, which begin on Christmas Eve and continue until January 6th, the celebration of Epiphany (the celebration of the Wise Men's visit)

C. Christmas is also the time that we hear and sing beautiful carols that praise God for sending His Son (look up some of the history of these carols—they have some fascinating stories!)

　　1. *Silent Night*

　　2. *Away in a Manger*

　　3. *O Little Town of Bethlehem*

4.   *Joy to the World*

5.   *O Come, All Ye Faithful*

6.   *Good Christian Men Rejoice*

7.   *The First Noël*

8.   *Angels We Have Heard on High*

9.   *Angels From the Realms of Glory*

10.   *Hark! The Herald Angels Sing*

11.   *It Came Upon a Midnight Clear*

12.   *We Three Kings of Orient Are*

13. *What Child is This?*

14. *O Holy Night*

D. Many American families celebrate this beautiful day with the same types of activities

1. Time is spent attending worship services

2. The family gathers together to exchange gifts and prepare a special meal together

3. The day is shared with family and loved ones, focusing on His birth

   a. Families often prepare a birthday cake for Baby Jesus

   b. Time is spent taking food or other items to others less fortunate

VIII. **Enjoy the study and remember that as time goes by, specifics and history can become a bit blurry, but the Reason for the season will always remain the same—Christ is born!**

Finish Line FUN!

I always try to complete a unit study with some kind of finale—a grand finish that is fun and rewarding, but which also showcases the children's efforts. To finish your Christmas unit study, use the space below to record your family's narration of what really happened at your Christmas celebration—the people that were there, the menu, the games, and all of the memorable events! Don't forget to include photos too!

Write about the people, places, food, games, and events of your celebration:

_____
_____
_____
_____
_____
_____
_____
_____
_____
_____
_____
_____
_____
_____
_____
_____
_____
_____
_____
_____
_____
_____
_____
_____
_____
_____
_____
_____
_____
_____

About The Author

Amanda Bennett, author and speaker, wife and mother of three, holds a degree in mechanical engineering. She has written this ever-growing series of unit studies for her own children, to capture their enthusiasm and nurture their gifts and talents. The concept of a thematic approach to learning is a simple one. Amanda will share this simplification through her books, allowing others to use these unit study guides to discover the amazing world that God has created for us all.

Science can be a very intimidating subject to teach, and Amanda has written this series to include science with other important areas of curriculum that apply naturally to each topic. The guides allow more time to be spent enjoying the unit study, instead of spending weeks of research time to prepare for each unit. She has shared the results of her research in the guides, including plenty of resources for areas of the study, spelling and vocabulary lists, fiction and nonfiction titles, possible careers within the topic, writing ideas, activity suggestions, addresses of manufacturers, teams, and other helpful resources.

The science-based series of guides currently includes the Unit Study Adventures titles:

Baseball	*Oceans*
Computers	*Olympics*
Elections	*Pioneers*
Electricity	*Space*
Flight	*Trains*
Gardens	*Dogs*
Home	

The holiday-based series of guides currently includes the Unit Study Adventures titles:

Christmas
Thanksgiving

This planned 40-book series will soon include additional titles, which will be released periodically. We appreciate your interest. "Enjoy the Adventure."